gary e. trawick

Give Them
Another Chance

gary e. trawick

Give Them Another Chance
gary e. trawick

The Country Bookshop

since 1953
Southern Pines, North Carolina

Give Them Another Chance

For information about permission to reproduce selections from this book
write to Permissions, The Country Bookshop,
140 NW Broad Street, Southern Pines, NC 28387

For information about special discounts for bulk purchases, please contact
Kimberly at The Country Bookshop 910.692.3211

Printing by Ingram Spark, Tennessee
Book Design by Judi Hewett
Cover art by Teresa D. Daniels
Production manager: Kimberly Daniels

Library of Congress Cataloging-in-Publication Data
Trawick Gary, author
Title: Give Them Another Chance/gary e. trawick
Description: First Edition | Southern Pines: The Country Bookshop, {2019}
ISBN 9780999131732
Essays, North Carolina
BISAC: LITERARY COLLECTIONS / Essays; HISTORY / Essay

ISBN 9780999131732-1 pbk.

The Country Bookshop
140 North West Broad Street
Southern Pines, North Carolina 28387

1 2 3 4 5 6 7 8 9 0

gary e. trawick

For Jennings

Who has put up with me for over a half century

Give Them Another Chance

gary e. trawick

AUTUMN

Your life may be in its autumn,

but winter is yet to come;

that some leaves may have fallen,

does not mean spring will not come.

So wrap your coat around you,

and face into the wind;

for you do not know how many summers,

before your life will end.

Yes, your steps may be slower,

and your eyes may be dim;

but there are still lots of prizes,

left for you to win!

gary e. trawick

gary e. trawick

Table of Contents

Table of Contents

Give Them Another Chance

Vestina

It was one of those late summer afternoons in the South when the sun had set and a gentle breeze was caressing the needles in the tops of the pines. I was sitting on the deck of a house in Columbia, South Carolina, and a few feet away sat an old woman deep in contemplation, sharing her thoughts with me.

The old woman sitting near me had deep lines in her face. Her hands were covered with brown liver spots. Her eyes were dim from cataracts. She could hear only with the aid of a little tan plastic voice magnification device inserted into her ear. There are people whose strength of character shows in their faces, and she was one of those people. The natural strength of personality had been made even stronger by raising a family during the Depression, hearing Taps blown for two sons killed in the military and living with and always loving a man who drank a little more than he should.

The old woman sitting across from me was Vestina Jarrett, my wife's grandmother. This was her day, her birthday; she was one hundred years old. The family had gathered in Columbia to celebrate. The plans were she would go to a nursing home in Columbia so she would be close to her daughter. She had never lived outside the mountains of North Carolina. She was a true product of the mountains, having been born there, married a boy from the mountains, made her home and raised her family in those mountains of which she was a part. You could sit on her front porch in Bandana and get her talking about the old days— she would look across the mountain and tell you she was raised in a hollow just on the other side. She would relate that as a young girl when she and Ralph were dating he would come for her on a horse and they would go off together on horseback. You got the feeling she wished people still rode horses, particularly since she never learned to drive an automobile.

It was unusual for her and me to have those few minutes alone that day. Her daughter was going to take her back to Bandana the next day to stay a couple of weeks before she entered the nursing home. I can still see Mrs. Jarrett looking out across the yard and asking questions that went like this: "Gary, when I go home if I were to get sick they would have to take me to a hospital in Spruce Pine, wouldn't they?"

"Well," I replied, "yes, I guess if you were sick, they wouldn't be able to bring you all the way back to Columbia."

Then she asked, "If the doctor in Spruce Pine felt I needed to stay close so he could look after me they would have to put me in a facility close to Spruce Pine, wouldn't they?"

Again I replied, "Well, yes ma'am, I suppose if the doctor wanted you close and if there was a place near Spruce Pine, that's what they would have to do."

Two weeks later my wife got a phone call from Betty, Mrs. Jarrett's daughter. She told my wife, "Mama is in the hospital. We had planned to come home on Sunday, but on Friday she started having severe stomach pains and the doctor felt he should keep her in the hospital for observation." About the end of the next week another phone call from Betty, "The doctor has found a vacancy at the local nursing home in

Spruce Pine and he would like for Mama to stay there for a while so he can keep an eye on her."

When I came home I could not help but laugh when my wife relayed the conversations with Betty to me. I had not told anyone about my conversation with Mrs. Jarrett on the deck.

While in the nursing home in Spruce Pine she shared a room with an eighty-two year old woman who was the widow of one of her son's friends. This woman could not walk or move around except in a wheelchair and Vestina and the woman worked out an arrangement. The woman read the Bible to Mrs. Jarrett, and Mrs. Jarrett pushed her around the nursing home in her wheelchair.

I wish she were still living so I could get her telling stories again about how life was when she was young. However, what I really wish is to get more lessons on how to keep control of my life as I get older.

Give Them Another Chance

One of the interesting aspects of being a trial judge is the opportunity it gives you to observe human behavior. Once in Williamston we were involved in the trial of four young men charged with armed robbery. They had decided to rob a "counting house". A counting house is the place where the organizers of a numbers racket gather to count the money that the runners bring in from selling illegal lottery tickets. They reasoned that if they robbed the counting house the victims would be unable to report it to the police as they also were engaged in illegal activity.

One stayed in the car to act as lookout and getaway driver. The other three with guns went to the house, two to the front door and one to the back. When the one in the back hollered the doors were kicked open and the boys rushed into the house only to find an elderly black couple watching television. Instead of just leaving, they persisted with their hooded faces to terrorize the old couple. The defendants fired several shots though the roof of the house.

The woman eventually went to her bedroom and brought out seventy-nine dollars and some change which she had in a sock. All the cash the couple had in the world.

As soon as they left, the old man called the police and gave a description of the robbers and within forty-five minutes they were apprehended. They had stopped at a convenience store and gone in the bathroom. The manager of the store became suspicious when the boys came out not wearing the same clothes they had on when they entered. He activated his silent alarm. The police arrested them before they could leave the premises.

They were before me for sentencing. I looked out into the courtroom and saw one whole row taken up by parents of the young boys. They were neat in appearance and their faces showed not only disappointment in their sons, but real fear of what might happen to them.

The law at that time required an active sentence of seven years without parole for a conviction of armed robbery. There was a catch in the law—if the defendant was less than twenty-one years of age, the judge in his discretion could sentence him as a "committed youthful offender". The status of CYO meant a defendant would be eligible for parole the day he entered the prison system. The lawyers for the young men argued for CYO status and the district attorney opposed CYO status.

Wanting input from the victims, I called upon them to see how they felt about sentencing. The courtroom became quiet. Everyone knew the fate of four young men depended upon what an elderly couple advised the court. I can still see that old man after I asked him what he felt I should do. Whether I should sentence them so they would be eligible for parole immediately, or whether I should sentence them so they would have to serve seven years in prison before becoming eligible. He leaned over to his wife and they whispered back and forth. I knew she would have to agree to whatever he told me. You could tell by their interaction they had lived together many more years than they had lived separately and had faced most of life's hardships and battles together.

Finally the old man rose from where they were seated and with the aid of a cane walked down the aisle of the courtroom to a spot directly in front of the bench. The fathers would not look at the old man. The mothers were just the opposite. They looked directly at the old man as he came down, almost it seemed as if trying to catch his eye. The look in each face was one of pleading, of begging. One mother had streaks down her face from tears that were dropping into her lap — making no effort to wipe them.

The old man was slightly bent, the wrinkles in his face showing obvious years of outside work. Yet there was a dignity about him that is possessed only by those with the character trait of humility. He looked me square in the eye and said: "Your Honor, these are young boys, give them another chance."

In a profession in which I observe more often the desire for vengeance and retribution, I was this day able to observe forgiveness beyond anything I could image. I had observed, first hand, forgiveness like that of Jesus.

Bill's Friend

My brother, Bill, was to come home one weekend and called to say he would be unable to do so. A friend had been robbed and severely beaten. He was in the hospital in critical condition. Bill was going to stay in Washington and sit with him in the hospital. He remained in critical condition for more than two weeks. His doctors had his family come from the midwest not knowing whether he would recover.

It was several months before Bill came home and I heard the full story. His friend had come home from work, entered his house and started to the back when a blow from a fireplace poker knocked him to the floor. Practically unconscious he began feeling around for his glasses with his hands. The intruder took delight in the realization that Bill's friend, without his glasses, was nearly blind.

The assailant would laugh as he would try to get away and run into furniture, knocking over tables, breaking lamps, tripping over ottomans. When he fell the intruder would strike him with the poker and taunt him to try to get away. Finally, even his poor eyesight detected an area of light, which he knew to be his living room window. He jumped through it, cutting himself, but securing his escape.

After several weeks the doctors turned their attention from his physical injuries to his mental injuries. Bill related that at night he would begin screaming as nightmares came and the voice and laughing of the assailant became as real as on the late afternoon when he heard them. Over and over he relived the horror.

As the time approached for him to be released, the doctors called his family together. They were advised that the emotional trauma and experience that he had suffered would require extensive counseling and should begin while he was still in the hospital.

The day came for his first session with the psychologist. The doctor began to question him: "Tell me, what feelings do you have about this person who did this to you?", asked the doctor.

"I have feelings of pity for him," replied Bill's friend.

"That's not possible, you must have feelings of anger or hatred or a desire for revenge or some such emotion has to be within you. It's only human," the doctor continued.

"No, I really do not have any of those emotions," Bill's friend replied.

"You cannot just shut this whole episode out of your life and pretend it did not happen," the doctor told him and continued, "Tell me, when you think about the person who did this to you, what thoughts go through your mind?"

"I was angry at first. I even hated him. Then as I lay in this hospital room I have had so many friends to come. So much of my family has stood by me. While in this hospital room I have felt nothing but the love of friends and family. Then one day it occurred to me that the person who did this to me is out there somewhere in the streets, probably all alone, while I am here surrounded by love from caring family and friends. I realized how much better off I am than he is. My only feelings for him are those of pity. My anger subsided, my hatred subsided and eventually went away completely, replaced by a feeling of thankfulness for how fortunate I am."

All of us have been recipients of love. We normally do not think of it as a cure but, as this young man demonstrated it often is. When we see people who are sick or hurting, we wish we were doctors. Perhaps we need only to exercise our ability to show love and compassion to be healers!

How to Get on a Pedestal

When lawyer groups meet these days there are two hotbutton issues that often are on the program. One is quality of life. Lawyers bemoan the fact that demands on the profession are such that the stress level has risen to the point that quality of life is not what they desire. A second issue is the regard the public has for the profession.

From articles I read I have come to realize these are also hotbutton issues among members of the medical profession. They go out into the world with the title lawyer or doctor attached to their names and often find themselves somewhat disillusioned when they discover the general population may not think as highly of them as they may think of themselves.

In recent years the pedestal of respect has eluded many in the judiciary. Judicial elections, more than anything, has changed the public's perception of the judiciary. A judge's office has quickly become just another political office, tarnished by the process of getting elected.

When I hear the groaning and moaning of lawyers about the loss of respect or read articles about doctors whining that the public does not understand them, the names of two men come to my mind. They are Judge Clifton L. Moore and Dr. W. I Taylor. Both lived their lives high on the pedestal of respect in our community. Both were actually "loved" by the people they served. Both understood that while a profession is not a calling, being admitted into the legal or medical profession is a privilege that with it carries responsibilities. There are business aspects to a profession, but the business part should be minor, and service to clients and patients should be the major focus.

Clifton Moore started out as a practicing attorney and later became District Attorney. As DA he prosecuted the Ku Klux Klan at a time when it was powerful and taking on the Klan was a dangerous undertaking. Judge Moore became a Superior Court judge and then a Justice of the North Carolina Supreme Court. When his son was admitted to the practice of law, Judge Moore advised him: "Son, you will enjoy practicing law. You will enjoy helping people. However, you will not enjoy charging people."

Ivy Taylor was almost like a god in our town. The following illustrates why. When you left Dr. Taylor's office after being treated, you were given a bill by Mary Wright Cantwell, his receptionist. However, if you did not pay the bill no action was ever taken. In fact, you never got another bill, as Dr. Taylor did not send out bills.

Near the end of his practice Dr. Taylor himself got sick and had to be out of the office for a while. While he was gone Mary Wright and his nurse, Harriet Blake, reviewed the books. They went to Dr. Taylor and said: "Ivey, do you realize there are several hundred thousand dollars on the books. We think we should try to collect some of this money."

Dr. Taylor, after thinking about it for a while responded, "Ok, you can send them one bill, but do not tell me anyone to whom you send one because I do not want it to affect the way I might treat them should I see them on the street or they come back to the office."

Mary Wright and Harriet sent out the bills and the money started pouring in. In fact, in only a few weeks they had collected in excess of seventy thousand dollars. Around Thanksgiving of that year they told Dr. Taylor of all the money they had collected. He looked at them, smiled and said, "I tell you what let's do. If we collect any more money I will just have to give most of it to the IRS. If I'm going to have to give it away I would rather give it to my patients. So just don't charge anyone for the month of December."

These were two men who lived their professional lives on a pedestal. Neither placed himself on a pedestal. Both were placed there by the people they served.

Burgaw Is My Home Town

Burgaw is my home town. I was raised here; I went off to school and when I finished I came home.

There are no Jews in Burgaw, never have been as long as I can remember — with one exception. When I was just a boy a Jewish man by the name of Brooks lived here. He was a merchant who ran a store by the name of E. Brooks Department Store on main street. Whenever anyone referred to him they always said E Brooks and I was a teenager before I realized the E was the initial of his first name. I never heard what his first name was and back then used to imagine it was Elijah or Elisa or Enoch. Since he was Jewish, certainly he would have one of those Biblical type names. It just couldn't stand for Edward or Elwood or some of the names of my friends at school.

I really don't remember what he looked like. Even if someone showed me a picture I don't think I would recognize him. I do remember he had gray hair, but other than that I have no real recollection of his features. But there is one thing I remember about him. He was a gentle man. When you are a boy and go into a store by yourself to spend your own money it makes you feel mighty grownup when the owner himself waits on you. I know I must have bought other things there, but I particularly remember buying a toboggan. It was a blue toboggan like sailors wore. It cost twenty-five cents and it was from that toboggan that I first came to understand what the color Navy Blue was. Mr. Brooks treated me just like I had bought a full suit of clothes and I guess I thought my purchase was at least that important.

I was aware almost from the time I knew of Mr. Brooks that there was something different about him. There were occasions he would leave our town for several weeks. When this would happen my parents would talk about it between themselves. Their conversation would have that quiet tone that they were talking grown-up talk that children wouldn't understand, that tone that makes children want to overhear what is being said. Their demeanor was always solemn, like when one prays out loud in church. From what I could overhear the only thing I learned was something terrible had happened, something too awful to talk about in normal tones had happened, had happened to Mr. Brooks's family.

When I was about ten Mr. Brooks made the last of these trips out of town. My parents discussed it in tones more relaxed and there was a hopefulness about them that gave me the freedom to ask where Mr. Brooks had gone. My mother explained he had gone to Europe to try to find his family. Naturally I inquired what she meant. I didn't understand how one lost his family. That's when I first learned about the Holocaust. My mother didn't use the term holocaust; it would be years later before I would become acquainted with the term and its ramifications. She simply explained that the Nazis had taken Mr. Brooks's wife and children and he had never seen or heard from them since. She explained Mr. Brooks was considering remarriage, but wouldn't do so without making one last effort to find his wife and children. At least to try to know if they were dead or if by some miracle they had escaped.

I do not know what Mr. Brooks learned on that last trip to Europe. I do know that shortly after he returned he married and left our town.

He may have left, but the images of that gentle man searching through Europe for his family remains with me. The horror of that time was made more real as I read as a college freshman Anne Frank's diary. Now we have the Holocaust Memorial in Washington and Schiendler's List to remind us. I need only to ride down Main Street and see where E. Brooks Department Store was.

I cannot comprehend millions and millions of people. But the man who sold me the navy toboggan is real. At ten years of age I didn't understand how a community would allow this to happen. I'm over seventy now, I'm older and wiser but, in truth, I still do not understand.

This is a story I sometimes tell young people in court who I think are truly sorry for what they have done. As is often the case, they think they will never be able to amount to anything because of their conviction.

Buffalo Nickel

One day I was in one of those moods where life seemed to be a dead-end street for me. Things were not going as I wanted. In fact, something had happened which I thought would alter my life from that point on and I would never be able to achieve many of my goals and dreams. That particular day I was jogging and happened to look down and saw a nickel lying on the ground. I picked it up and saw it was a waafter 1938. This one was so worn that the date had been rubbed off. On one side was the imagine of an Indian. On the other was the imagine of a buffalo. You may not have seen one as the stopped making them in 1938.

As I jogged along I began thinking of the Indian as I held the coin in my hand. You see, when I was a little boy, I wanted to be an Indian. When the other kids wanted to be cowboys, I wanted to be an Indian. I would even tell my playmates that I was at least part Indian. It was only after I was older that I realized I could never be an Indian. That was not one of life's options that was available to me.

As I jogged farther along, feeling even more depressed, I began to think of the buffalo on the back of the coin. I began to think of how many buffalo there used to be and how few there are today. I thought that was sort of like my life- - I used to have many opportunities, but now they seemed so limited.

As I thought more deeply about the Indian, the buffalo, and my life, realism set in. Two important truths penetrated my depression.

I like to hunt and fish and I like to hunt and fish alone. My friends and family don't understand this. They don't understand why I will go down the river and fish all by myself or why I will pack my tent and sleeping bag and go out in the river swamps and camp all alone. They don't understand that when I do that I am actually an Indian. It's my chance to still be an Indian. I may never be a real Indian, but I can still dream.

I realized that not all the buffalo were gone. I also realized that buffalo were not the only animals you could hunt. There were more buffalo left than I could ever hunt and so many other animals that I did not even know their names. There were still more opportunities to accomplish the goals of my life than I could ever take advantage of, and there were many opportunities of which I was not even aware. If I just started looking I could fill up several lifetimes.

When life is dark, you need to remember your dreams. When it seems life has passed you by, you need to access all your opportunities — those to accomplish what you have heretofore thought you wanted and opportunities for things you have never before considered.

88 To Nothing

Wallace-Rose Hill was the archrival of Burgaw High. I was a sophomore at Burgaw. The year was 1960 and the Red Devils had not won
a football game in two years. I have never understood why someone
chose Wallace for our homecoming game. It just seems to me that
homecoming should be a happy occasion, and the prospect of beating
the Bulldogs never seemed to make for a happy occasion.

It was a perfect football night. It was October, just cool enough for
the cheerleaders to need to wear the wool athletic jackets of their player
boyfriends. There had been the usual homecoming parade downtown,
the picking of a homecoming queen, and the planning of the big dance
after the game.

Kenneth Futch ran the Esso service station in Burgaw. He was the
father of Kenneth Futch, Jr., whom we called Kenny Boy, who was also
a sophomore member of the team. He was also the husband of the high
school algebra teacher. He was the most rabid Burgaw Red Devil fan in
the town. He was a devout Methodist and while that did not make him
the equal of a backslidden Baptist, it did put his operation of the time
clock beyond question.

Wallace won the toss and elected to receive. The teams lined up,
the center placed the ball on the tee, the fans stood for the kickoff, the
cheerleaders were hollering and waving their pompoms in the air, the

whistle blew and the kicker ran to the ball and sent it down field to the twenty-yard line. About ten seconds later all the referees had their hands pointing to the sky, signaling the first touchdown for Wallace. During the first half this would be repeated eight more times.

The coach did not even come into the locker room at halftime. There was no cheering from the Red Devil side as we left the field. The only cheering came from the Wallace-Rose Hill side, which was a steady and loud chant of "we want a hundred, we want a hundred, we want a hundred."

The second half is when Kenneth Futch, in spite of his devout Methodism, in total disregard of being the husband of one of the most respected teachers of the high school, putting aside his role model responsibility to his son, yielded to temptation to help the Red Devils. During the second half of play he never allowed the clock to stop. It ran after incomplete passes, it ran after Bulldog touchdowns, it even ran during time-outs. When the final whistle blew, the score stood at eighty-eight to nothing. The Bulldogs didn't make a hundred because the timekeeper was on the side of the Red Devils.

It is easy to think no good can come from such total humiliation. I can without equivocation tell you I learned one of life's most important lessons that night. During my life I have attempted things that appeared from the beginning to be doomed to failure. Sometimes it was lawsuits in which it appeared I had no chance of winning. It was so the first time I ran for political office, me coming from a little small county and running against a candidate in the big neighboring county. It was true the time I set out to build a sailboat in my backyard. People would say, "You can't win, you're going to be humiliated." When I hear these comments I simply smile and inside say, "You just don't understand.

When you have lost a homecoming game to your archrival eighty-eight to nothing, life simply cannot hold any humiliation greater than that."

I often tell young lawyers that I never learned much from the cases I won. It is the cases I lost that taught me the most. My junior and senior years our team had respectable seasons and won some games. However, the most I learned from football about life came from a score of eighty-eight to nothing.

Kite Flying

I flew a kite more than a mile high. It's the truth. I know it is hard to believe, but I really did. My mother was right there. She would hold the balls of string and when I would put one ball out, she would hand me another ball. It was June 1956 and I was in the final round of the North Carolina Jaycees Kite Flying Contest.

More than a mile high! You think that's not possible, but it is. You see, I was more than a mile high when I started letting the string out. For the final contest we flew our kites off the mile-high swinging bridge at Grandfather Mountain, North Carolina. So while it may not be exactly as I led you to believe, it's still the truth — that I flew a kite more than a mile high.

I was thinking about that time not long ago. I'm over seventy and I still have a tradition of flying a kite every year. Flying a kite is sort of like life. Each time you fly a kite is different. Just like every day of life is different.

If it is a relatively calm day it takes a lot of effort to get a kite flying. You use a short tail and sometimes you need to run with the kite in order to create your own wind. Once the kite gets off the ground it will pick up wind, as there is always a little breeze blowing once you get thirty to fifty feet above the earth. Life's like that. Often times it is hard to get started. You just cannot seem to make much headway. It takes a lot of effort to get going. Once you do, the successes come easier and easier, and pretty soon you are flying high.

There are other days you go out to fly a kite and the wind is simply blowing too hard. Wind is coming against the kite just like life sometimes comes against us. Life can be so hard it can tear us to pieces, just like the wind can tear a kite to pieces. The only way to fly a kite in hard wind is to have a long tail to anchor the kite and give it stability. You also need stronger string to keep the kite from breaking loose. In life we need to keep connected to basic principles. When you get way up it is easy to think you have it made and there is no way you could nose dive and come crashing back to earth. However, it is most often when we are flying high, when we are soaring, that the strong winds come and cause us to crash.

Another similarity between kites and life is that both need to be flexible. If the ribs of a kite are too rigid it will not fly. Even if a kite with rigid ribs gets off the ground, the first strong wind will cause one of them to break and the skin of the kite loses its tautness and the kite simply flutters in the wind and drops back to the ground.

It is hard to argue against having strong opinions or convictions. We are taught to stand for something and not be tossed about by every wind that blows. However, life changes just as the winds change, and there are times when we need to be flexible and bend with it. While the ribs of a kite need to be flexible, the line or string that connects it to the earth has to always remain tight. You let the line get slack and the kite will lose altitude. In life there are convictions that must be held tight, and those that require some flexibility. We need the wisdom to know the difference.

Sometimes when you are flying a kite on a particularly good day and you just keep adding string until the kite looks almost like a little dot. Sometimes on these days it brings satisfaction to just let the kite go at the end of the day. Let it flutter off to some unknown place flying all on its own. In life we need also to know when to let go. This is particularly true with children. There are times when we need to keep the lines short, to keep them close where we can pull them back if a strong wind comes. Yet there comes a time with children when we need to let go. A time when we need to say to ourselves and to them — I've raised you off the ground — I've got you flying. Now you are on your own!

How Mama Doctors A Cut

I got hurt a lot growing up. I liked to be outside and I liked to play with knives and hatchets and saws. Getting cut was a fairly ordinary occurrence.

If my mama saw my cuts, I knew what was coming. She was going to clean the cut with alcohol and then put iodine on it. Since both alcohol and iodine would sting, actually I said burned, I would try to not let Mama know. If it was a minor scratch, it wouldn't make much difference. However, if I had really hurt myself, my hiding it from Mama often had long-term consequences. The cut would scab over, but underneath infection would set in. The skin around the scab would turn red and sometimes pus would ooze out from beneath the scab. Often the pain associated with the infection was worse than the cut.

Sooner or later Mama would see the sore or it would get to hurting so badly I would have no choice but to show it to her. She would say it looked "angry". The first thing she would do was fuss at me for not telling her so she could have doctored it before it got infected. Then she would try to medicate, but the hard scab would keep the medicine from reaching the infection. It would take a lot longer to heal.

Once I kept a deep cut on my leg, which had become infected, hidden from Mama so long the infection spread from my knee to my ankle. There were red streaks running up and down the calf of my leg. It was so bad Mama didn't even fuss at me; she just took me to Dr. Taylor's office. He lanced the wound, opened it up so the pus could run out, and put some salve on it. I thought he would put a bandage on it, but he explained to get well it needed the healing properties of being exposed to fresh air.

Recently I was involved in a series of church meetings at a church that had a significant controversy. One faction of the church felt decisions were made without their being able to express their viewpoint. The other faction, feeling the direction was best for the church, saw no reason to have a lot of discussion. Soon a scab grew over the problem and infection set in. No one, from either side, wanted to talk about it, but the problem was still there. Every so often the pus of hard feelings would ooze around the scab. As Mama would say, the sore was getting angrier and angrier. Being good Christian people, rather than hurt any feelings, they just wanted the problem to go away. Just as I, as a kid, hoped my cuts would heal without medicine.

When Mama would clean my cut, she would blow to relieve what I called burning from the iodine. Later, I learned the blowing really didn't help, but the fact Mama cared enough to try to do something did help.

I don't know how the church problem will eventually play out. However, I do know the problem has been made worse by the effort to hide it. It may heal by itself, but I doubt it. It is a deep cut and not a scratch. Sooner or later they will have to peel back the scab and expose the problem. When they do, the pain is going to be sharp.

If the church would apply Mama's process for treating cuts to treating their problems, they would:

First, treat problems early, before they get infected.

Second, try to clean the extraneous stuff from the hurt. Remove those things that really aren't important but prevents a focus on the true cause.

Third, apply medication. Seek solutions that can bring about healing, even though they might cause temporary pain.

Fourth, if necessary, seek professional help. And finally, blow the breath of love on the hurt.

Basketball In The Park

My job as a Superior Court judge often gives me unexpected free time. This afternoon was such a time. We finished jury selection around three o'clock but could not begin testimony until the next morning. I rode over to Southern Pines from Sanford to check out a kayak store I had heard about.

As the store closed my stomach was telling me it was suppertime. If you eat on the road a lot you get tired of the chains and fast food places. Plus, who wants to eat alone in some upscale restaurant with everyone around you being festive and laughing?

It was a perfect beginning of a fall afternoon. Temperature just right, leaves beginning to turn; you just wanted to be outside. Southern Pines has a little park right in the middle of the village. As I walked by it the idea struck me, I would eat here. So I went to one of those high-end grocery stores, the kind where they sell all sorts of fresh stuff. I bought the makings of a picnic.

A vacant bench beside a basketball court became my dining location. Before I even began to eat I started watching the kids playing ball. They appeared to range in age from teens to late twenties, all were black except for one white kid. One kid was confined to a wheelchair.

As I ate I became more and more engrossed in watching the kids. I thought that there was more to be learned here than how to play ball.

Here's some of what I thought:

(1)   Some kids came in new expensive cars and some in old ones with their bumpers blacked by exhaust — the type car you drive has nothing to do with how well you can shoot a basketball.

(2)   If someone made a shot, everyone who got the rebound threw it back to him — sort of like life: the more you succeed the more chances you get.

(3)   Every so often someone would throw the ball to the kid in the wheelchair; he would shoot and if he made it they would throw it to him again — maybe that's the way to treat handicapped folks, give them a chance to compete as best they can, reward them when they do well, but don't really show them too much favoritism.

(4)   A few of the kids brought balls, but most did not — if you have your own ball you can shoot goals, but you have to have other kids to play a game.

(5)   A big overweight kid was the best shot — if you judge people's ability by their looks you just might misjudge them.

(6)   All the kids looked different — some wore baggy pants I thought might drop to their knees at any second while others had athletic shorts; some had neat haircuts while others had hair in their eyes. However, when the game was going, they all played by the same rules — you do not have to look the same to play by the same rules.

(7)   No one eating in one of those upscale restaurants had a more perfect meal than I — which just goes to show that if the atmosphere is perfect the food can be less than perfect.

(8)   Once the ball came rolling over to where I was sitting and a boy came running to get it. I picked it up and when he saw me he stopped and when I threw it to him he said "thank you". I thought politeness

still reigns — if a person wants to help, let them, but say "thank you".

(9)   The white kid was accepted and treated like everyone else — if you are pursuing a common goal, skin color doesn't seem to make much difference.

(10)   Everybody had a chance to shoot — that's what is important in life: a chance.

I was hearing a first-degree capital murder case that week. The defendant was twenty-three and the evidence was he had no home life and few friends. I could not help wondering what a difference it might have made if he could have played basketball in the park.

Johnny's Visit

I had a visit from Johnny Morellis last week. Well, I know you will figure out before I finish that Johnny Morellis is not his real name. However, I promise you the person is real and what I'm going to tell you about him also is real.

Johnny and I are not really friends; acquaintances would be a better term. He was in school with me, though a few years younger.

I got a call from a mutual friend who said Johnny wanted to talk with me about some legal problems. He said Johnny didn't feel he could call me directly, but really needed some help. I told him I was no longer practicing law and as a judge I really could not give legal advice. He said Johnny couldn't afford to pay a lawyer and would I please give him a few minutes. I told him I would be in my study the next afternoon and to tell Johnny to come by around five o'clock.

My study is over our garage and I heard Johnny's car in the drive. In a couple of minutes he was climbing the short flight of stairs to the study. He stopped about halfway up to catch his breath and stopped again at the top to catch his breath a second time. He looked over at me and smiled, a smile coming from a gaunt face with slightly sunken eyes. Johnny had never been a big man, but his frame seemed even smaller and his shoulders seemed to bow inward. It didn't take a doctor to tell me Johnny was seriously ill.

We talked about people we both knew and about Burgaw High School days. Finally, we talked about his legal problems. I had already figured out what was wrong with Johnny, but I asked him anyway. He told me he was dying of complications from AIDS. He had been fighting the disease for years, but in the last year he seemed to be losing. He had quit work and was living on social security disability.

I asked him why he did not come home where there would be family to help care for him. He smiled and replied, "I would be an embarrassment to my family."

I said, "Go to Wilmington, you used to live there, it is close."

"I cannot get the help there I can where I live, "he replied. He went on to explain his meager income could not pay for his medication. That the larger cities of the Piedmont had programs to help defer the medical costs.

"What about the churches?" I asked, "Certainly Wilmington churches offer help for people suffering as you are."

A hollow laugh came from deep inside him, "Most churches don't want a gay person to even darken the doors, must less offer us help."

Johnny left my physical presence that afternoon, but he did not leave me mentally. I called about a dozen of the larger churches in Wilmington and asked if they could help with money for medication for someone with AIDS. No church said they could. Several referred me to social services.

I'm not a theologian and I don't understand all that God approves and disapproves, and when you forgive and when you are tolerant. I'm not a psychologist and I don't understand what makes a person gay or straight. I do understand suffering, because I have experienced it and I have seen it. I saw it that afternoon in the face of Johnny Morellis. Not only the suffering caused by the pain of his sickness, but the suffering of loneliness and rejection; the suffering, of hopelessness.

I thought about that old 60s folk song: "Where have all the flowers gone-long time passing-gone to young girls everyone when will they ever learn." I thought maybe there needed to be a new verse:

"Where have all the Christians gone, long time passing? Where have all the Christians gone, long time ago? Where have all the Christians gone? Gone to churches everyone, when will they ever learn? When will they ever learn?

Pregnant

"So, how has life been treating you," I asked.

"Good, really good," she answered then continued as she patted her stomach, "I just keep getting bigger." She had been looking straight ahead as we walked down the sidewalk toward the little cafe where we were going for lunch, but now she turned to look me in the face, "I'm pregnant." With this announcement she turned away from me and looked down the street again, but I could feel her eyes cut toward me and I knew she was searching my face for my reaction.

I wasn't quite sure what to say and just blurted out, "Well, is this something you are happy about?"

"Oh, I'm very happy. I'm over thirty and wanted a child for a long time," she replied.

"And what about the father?" I inquired, "Is he happy?"

"He offered to marry me, but then in the same breath said he was having feelings for an old girlfriend. I told him life was too short for him to get hooked up with me and spend his life wishing he was with someone else. If he is in town he stops by and we go eat or something-nothing else. He says he will send support."

"What do your folks think about all this?" I asked.

"Well, they are all pretty mad with me," she answered,

"Except my granddaddy, I think he has forgiven me."

We had gotten together that day because she had agreed to help me with a project. She is an artist and she is good at what she does. We have known each other a long time, but are not close friends. Casual friends would be a better description. Even so I felt my reaction to her situation mattered to her.

We were joined by one of her friends and the conversation became generic. As the time came for me to leave, her friend turned to speak to someone else, and I looked her in the face and said, "I'm not judgmental."

She held my gaze a few seconds before saying, "Thanks."

I spend a lot of time driving from court to court and it gives me time to think. I have thought a lot about her and what I would like to say to her. I cannot tell her I approve of getting pregnant on purpose without being married. It's not what you might think, religious reasons. It's that when people asked me what the hardest job in the world is, I instantly say, "being a single parent". My wife and I have three children and I cannot in my wildest imagination fathom what it would have been like to try to raise them alone. My wife agrees even though she could have come closer than me to doing it.

Just think, in four months there will be a new little person in the world. It will be so full of potential. It might create beautiful things like its mother does that bring happiness to people. There is no limit to the good it might do.

Of course, it will have the potential to do bad things. How it turns out depends on so many things, but being loved and cared for will have a great deal to do with it. I know its mother and I know she will love it, maybe too much. But what about the rest of us? Will we be accepting? Will we hold it against the child that the mother violated society's norms?

I believe the love of a parent prepares a child to expect and give love to all the world. I further believe it is the worst of sins for society to kill that expectation of love that exists within the child. Children are the responsibility of us all.

When she was searching my face for signs of my judgment of her, I wish I had asked if she remembered the story from the Bible about the men bringing to Jesus the woman caught in adultery. They were going to stone her, but first wanted to know what Jesus thought. The story goes that Jesus wrote something in the dirt and then said, "Let he who is without sin, cast the first stone." If I had been in the group that day, I would have had to drop my rock and gone home.

A Good Woman

Sometimes life comes against us in a hard way. Often it is the result of our own actions or maybe our not doing what we should that would have prevented it.

This last category is often the case with young people who appear in front of me in criminal court. Many times I can see in their face they believe their lives are ruined; they have no future. Often times when I have a young man in front of me who I can sense is really remorseful-who is really sorry; I like to tell him the story of a man I know.

When he was in high school he was a star athlete, particularly in football. He was good enough to be given a full ride to one of our major universities on a football scholarship. In the spring of his freshman year he was riding around one night with some boys — drinking, carousing as it used to be called. One of the boys suggested they rob a motel they had passed. This boy had the gumption to say "no"; he was not going to be part of a robbery. However, he didn't have the gumption to say, "Let me out". He stayed in the car while the other boys went in and robbed the motel. They were quickly caught and this boy was charged right along with the others. He escaped active prison time but spent several years on probation. He lost his athletic scholarship and dropped out of college.

I did not know the man during this period of his life. When I got to know him he was a pillar of his church, held a high position with one of the departments of state government, and was respected by all who knew him.

I have tried to analyze why he turned around. What was it that allowed him to overcome the stupidity of that night? Some would say it was because he got involved in church. Some would say it was because he loved his children so much, he would do nothing to disappoint them. Some would say he was trying to regain the love of his parents, but he knew his parents would love him regardless.

I've got my own theory. He got to going with and married a good woman. Men are quick to give women credit for raising children, but we are not too quick to give women credit for our personal successes. My brother, Ross, was an exception. He used to tell me that if he and I had not married the women we did, we would have been so sorry Mama would not have claimed us.

I'm sure the church, his children, and his parents all played a part. But it was this good woman who got him involved in church, this good woman who bore him children, this good woman who insisted that while they had established their own family, the relationship with parents should be maintained.

No, I don't tell these young boys in front of me that the secret to getting on the right road is to run out and get married. I do tell them they are at a crossroads and within the next few years they will make three decisions that will chart the remainder of their lives.

First is what they decide to do to earn enough of this world's material goods to support themselves. About one-third of each day is going to be spent doing this and they need to choose carefully.

Second is who or what their god is. There is no such thing as not having a god. They may not refer to it as a god, but it will be a god nevertheless. It will be whatever they put their faith in to support themselves in hard times. It may be money, it may be high social standing, it may be their job or it may be their family. It may be the God of creation worshiped in most churches. They need to choose carefully.

And the third decision is whom they choose as their life's mate. There are those few people who never feel the need to make a commitment to another human being, to forge a family unit and face life together. I cannot imagine facing some of the times I've gone through without my wife. They must to choose carefully.

The man I use as an example chose a good woman and I believe it has made all the difference.

Little Miss Mary

Last week I was wandering around in the cemetery. It's something I do occasionally. I know it sounds weird, maybe even morbid. My wife thinks so. I came across Mary Taylor's marker. Little Miss Mary is what most of us called her.

Little Miss Mary Taylor who was less than five feet tall and weighed less than ninety pounds. She was an old maid school teacher who taught first grade for more than forty years.

Little Miss Mary Taylor who was the daughter of a Baptist preacher. Preached in a bunch of the churches in Pender County before the Lord up and called him to some little town in west Texas.

Little Miss Mary Taylor who one night at church conference when the deacons and the preacher were telling the folks about as how we needed to be making plans for the big population explosion that was coming, with Wilmington being full and all, said she had been hearing about this population explosion for twenty years and hadn't seen it yet. Said we had enough problems right now that needed tending to without worrying ourselves too much about those Wilmington folks spilling over across the river.

Little Miss Mary Taylor who after she retired ran a two inch by three inch advertisement each week in the local paper that read: "Anyone who wants to know how to become a Christian call" and then had her phone number.

Most folks assumed Miss Mary never had any fun — certainly not the type fun ordinary people have. Her neighbors Jewell and Margaret Harrell knew better. She loved to play Scrabble and they said she could be vicious in her desire to win.

Little Miss Mary Taylor who never learned to drive an automobile. Lived only a block from the school so she walked. After she retired you could see her walking in her pink dress the half-mile or so to the hospital where she would sit and give out visitor cards.

Little Miss Mary Taylor who said she did not know whether homosexuality was a sin — thought it probably was. But she could not vote to exclude them from church because she was afraid they might be born that way and she would have to answer in judgment for denying them access to the gospel. Truth be known she would rather exclude folks for drinking alcohol. Thought the devil came right out of a beer bottle. Wouldn't rent a building her family owned in town to a grocery store because they were going to sell beer. When they offered to buy she wouldn't sell unless they put a clause in the deed they wouldn't sell beer. The sale fell through and they finally sold the building to the county for about half the money.

Little Miss Mary Taylor who got a burden for children in Mexico. When she died the bulk of her estate went for mission work in Mexico. It was more than a hundred thousand dollars-all from a little woman who lived on a teacher's salary her whole adult life.

Little Miss Mary Taylor who left her body to East Carolina Medical school so the students there could dissect it or whatever they do to learn anatomy. When they finished cutting on it they cremated what was left and sent it back to me in a little plastic box. Larry "Big Red"

Johnson, a man in the church, made a box out of heart pine and we put her ashes in it and buried them beside her mama and daddy in the town cemetery.

Little Miss Mary Taylor who had two favorite relatives, a nephew and a niece. The nephew was a colonel in the army- graduated West Point. He gave Miss Mary one of those green metal ammo boxes which she kept in the back of her closet. She kept cash money in it she used to give to the needy. Mostly gave it to young folks other people in town thought were misfits or delinquents. The niece visited Miss Mary often and would take her to church. The niece wore big hats and the little girls would ask their mothers if she was rich or a movie star.

Little Miss Mary Taylor, I guess her life didn't amount to much. No one erected a monument to her. Her portrait doesn't hang in any public building. No one has written a book about her. Of course those thousand or so people she taught to read and write and do arithmetic might beg to differ. Not a few of them became teachers themselves. One even got a PhD and is a professor in some college out west. Some have served on the town board and some on the county commission.

Little Miss Mary Taylor whose grave marker is just sixteen by twenty inches. Only has her name and the date she was born and the date she died. Little Miss Mary Taylor, if she had just been bigger, maybe her life would have counted for something.

Granddaddy and Uncle Leaman

The first time I remember seeing Uncle Leaman I was eight years old. I was staying with my grandparents in the part of the country where Alabama, Georgia and Florida join. They had a little farm and granddaddy, whom everyone called Uncle Charlie, ran a country store. My older brother and I would spend our summers with them.

It was late at night. I had already gone to bed when I heard someone at the door. I eased out and slipped to where I could see granddaddy talking with a black man. He went out and I went to grandmamma to see what it was all about.

She told me: "He needs something from the store. Go back to bed." Something in the tone of her voice made me know something out of the ordinary was going on. I slept in the back room, next to the washroom and it was easy for me to slip out without anyone knowing. There was a fig tree about thirty feet from the back door of the store and I eased around and hid in it.

Uncle Leaman's old pickup was backed up to the door and they were loading something into it. They worked without speaking, their movements purposeful, deliberate. Uncle Leaman pulled a canvas cover over the pickup bed when the last of the bags had been loaded.

I heard granddaddy tell him to wait just a minute and disappear into the store. When he came back he had two bottles- one brown, the other green. I watched as granddaddy handed Uncle Leaman the brown bottle and he put it to his lips and tilted his head back. He then took the 7-up bottle from granddaddy and chased the gulp of whiskey. He handed the bottles to granddaddy and he did the same — first the whiskey and then the 7-up.

The men looked at each other, smiled, and then broke into a big laugh. Without saying anything Uncle Leaman got into his pickup and headed down the sandy road. Granddaddy sauntered back to the house to a woman anxiously waiting, not having approved of what I had just seen.

It would be years before I fully comprehended all that I had seen. Before I realized I had witnessed the law being broken by my granddaddy selling sugar to a bootlegger. More important that I had witnessed a cultural taboo being broken — a white man having a social drink with a black man, particularly since he had allowed the black man to drink first and had put his lips to the same bottle as the black man.

The last time I saw Uncle Leaman was about ten years later. My family was sitting in the dining room of my grandparents' house. It was the day of granddaddy's funeral. My Aunt Inez went to the door in response to a knock. From my seat I could see Uncle Leaman in a blue suit, white shirt and tie and wearing a gray felt hat. His wife and children were with him. My aunt came to the table and said something I could not hear to my daddy who went out. Everyone at the table was looking at Aunt Inez, waiting for an explanation of what was going on.

With a sad smile she said, "Uncle Leaman wants to see daddy."

I excused myself from the table and went to the back bedroom. I eased out through the washroom as I had ten years earlier. The church was only two hundred feet from the house and I could see daddy leading Uncle Leaman and his family to the church. When they got to the front door I saw daddy speak with an usher. After their short exchange of words daddy led the group around to a side door.

I rushed to the church and went in the front door. Standing there I watched as daddy took Uncle Leaman to stand at granddaddy's coffin. Uncle Leaman held his hat in his left hand and I saw that big, rough, right hand-the same hand that had held the whiskey bottle, wipe his eyes. They stayed only a few minutes and left.

I intercepted daddy on the way back to the house. We didn't speak at first. I couldn't stand it any longer and had to ask: "Why didn't Uncle Leaman just come to the funeral?"

Daddy did not look at me. After some hesitation he said, "They just don't do that down here." The reality would come to me that they just didn't do that in Burgaw either.

Sitting in church less than an hour later, the truth of just how segregated a society I lived in came upon me. It had never seemed wrong before. After all, it was just the way it was. One thing I knew for certain — granddaddy would have liked for Uncle Leaman to have been there.

Resolutions

Well, it's New Year's Day. Another year is here. If you have not already done so, it's time to make your resolutions. I know you say you don't make resolutions because you never keep them. Well, that's a fine attitude. Maybe you shouldn't go to school because you just might fail. Don't get married, it might end in divorce. And for crying out loud don't have children as they just grow up and leave home! Maybe that last statement isn't true, which could be even worse, they just might not leave home.

Faithfully, each year I make resolutions. I've even developed a form on which I make my resolutions. I make ten. The first two have to do with my spiritual life. The next five have to do with self-improvement and personal goals. The last three have to do with relationships with family and friends.

Once made and written down, I put the list somewhere I will run across it several times during the year. I have just been reviewing some from past years. No, I have not kept them all. Truth is, I haven't kept most of them. But there are some I have kept and a few I have turned into habits. Just looking at some of them I can give you an example of the type resolutions I make. That does not mean they would be right for you, or that you even need improvement in these areas.

Under spiritual I don't make great big ones like I'm not going to sin or I'm going to read everything written by C. S. Lewis, though I might resolve to read one C. S. Lewis book. It's more like I'm going to read my Sunday School lesson each week or maybe I'm going to say a blessing each time I eat even if I'm by myself. One year I made a resolution to read the Bible from Genesis to Revelations and kept it. Most of them I keep only for a while and then slip.

In the personal improvement and goals group, instead of having five I need five hundred, but I put only five. Looking at past lists some of them have been repeats almost every year — like losing ten pounds. Now that's one I have achieved as often as three times in one year. Lose ten-gain ten-lose ten-gain them back. Exercise is a big one in this group. One that's been on the list for several years is to complete writing a history of Pender County. I'm glad to say I have finally met that one. One I'm renewing this year is to go somewhere for an overnight at least once a month. It doesn't have to be New York or somewhere fancy — maybe camping on Black River. A new one for this year is to get a colonoscopy like my doctor has been advising me to do for the past five years. You get the drift of the type things I resolve.

In the family and friends group there are such resolutions as the one two years ago to take my mother out to eat at least once a week. I've managed to keep it at least forty weeks out of the year. I resolved if I had not seen my brother in Charleston in two weeks to call him so we had some contact every two weeks. If I had made and kept the same resolution about my older brother who died, I would have saved myself a lot of guilt when we suddenly lost him long before it was time. I have a group of close friends, and we all have resolved to get together and cook and eat at least once a month and to take a trip somewhere each year. This year we did two, one fishing on the Outer Banks and the other to

Washington with our wives along.

So, get out your paper and pen. Make some resolutions! Don't make them all so grandiose there is no chance you will keep them. On the other hand, it's okay to have a couple of sliders, ones you know you can achieve-like the colonoscopy. Go ahead, make them, I dare you. Who knows, you may just keep a couple!

Love One Another

I was engaged in a conversation with an Arabic acquaintance, a Muslim. The conversation drifted to religion and he started trying to tell me that his was superior to mine. He knew I attended one of the protestant churches in town because I had once asked him if he would come to my church and talk about the Islamic religion after the 9/11 attack.

He knew the churches in Burgaw had few, and most not any, ethnic members. He was using this as an example of how we could not really be right with God when we were not open to all people. He told me how at the services at his mosque there were white, black, oriental and Middle Eastern people worshiping together.

Our conversation changed and a few minutes later we came to the war in Iraq. He saw the war as an attack against Islam, a religious war. Then even deeper, truer feelings emerged as he said, now almost ranting, "Anywhere in the world you find trouble, just look and you will find a Jew." He looked at me and continued, "It's been true since all of history, you find trouble, you find a Jew." I smiled at him and he laughed. He knew he had just blown his earlier sermon about how Islam was open to all.

I thought about a conversation I had had about a month earlier with a staff member of a Christian church. We were talking also about the war in Iraq. He knew I was not convinced our invasion was justified and l did not buy into the reasons given by the government for going to war.

He looked me straight in the eye and with as much feeling and with as much honesty of belief my Arabic acquaintance had told me about Jews being in the midst of any world trouble he asked, "Don't you believe it is God's will we go to Iraq? Don't you think God wants us to confront Islam?"

l am not a theologian. Maybe someone needs to explain to me how the Jews who claim the God of Abraham, Isaac and Jacob as their God and the Muslims who claim the God of Abraham, Isaac and Jacob as their God and Christians who claim the God of Abraham, Isaac and Jacob as their God can have such ill feeling toward each other over their religious beliefs that they justify killing each other. If Jesus and the Father are one and both have existed from the beginning of time, this means Jesus was there as the God of Abraham, Isaac and Jacob at the beginning of the Jewish, Islamic and Christian religions.

A verse from the Koran, the holy book of the Muslims, says, "Do good to parents, kinsfolk, orphans, the neighbor who is near of kin, the neighbor who is a stranger, the companion by your side, and the wayfarer. . ."

A verse from Leviticus, part of the holy book of both the Jews and the Christians says: "But the stranger that dwelleth with you shall be unto you as one born among you, and thou shalt love him as thyself . . ."

A verse from the Christian Bible says: "Thou shall love thy neighbor as thyself."

All three verses command we love and do good to our neighbors. All three religions contend they are commands from the God of Abraham, Isaac and Jacob.

Today is Maundy Thursday. It is the day Christians remember that last earthly gathering of Jesus and his disciples. That night they broke bread together and drank wine together and he washed their feet. The word Maundy is of doubtful origin, but probably comes from a Hebrew word meaning commandment.

It was on this night Jesus said:" A new commandment I give unto you, that ye love one another." Maybe that is still the message for this Maundy Thursday and perhaps for this Easter season — that Christians, Muslims and Jews love one another. That we all follow the command of the God of Abraham, Isaac and Jacob-the God of the Jews, the Muslims, and the Christians that we do good to and love our neighbors.

Old Enough

Some years ago I was invited to make a talk to a civic club. Before the meeting they had a meal. As I passed the opening from the kitchen to the dining area I saw someone I knew and spoke to him. As I moved away where I'm sure they thought I could not hear them, I heard a woman ask: "Was that Judge Trawick?"

The man to whom I had spoken replied, "Yes."

The woman's response in a surprised voice was, "Good gracious, I didn't know he was that old!"

Well, I didn't think I was old, much less, looked old. When I got to the table I put my plate down and said I was going to wash my hands. To tell the truth I wanted to look in the mirror--you know, to see if I had changed much since I had shaved that morning.

Not only had I never thought about the fact someone might think I was old, I had never contemplated the possibility I might one day be old. I mean I was going so fast when I turned forty that I was at least forty-five before I realized I was not still in my thirties.

I guess the next time I really realized I just might not always be frozen in my high school graduation body was right after I passed the big five-o. I decided I was going to go to some doctors and really get checked out. I mean, instead of just getting my routine physical, I was going to get my eyes checked, my hearing checked, my teeth checked, and get my regular Doc to run some extra tests. I made all the appointments and started making the rounds of the medical community.

Let me tell you, by the time I finished I needed one more appointment — a psychiatrist. I was depressed. No, they didn't find anything serious wrong with me. As I got ready to get out of the dentist's chair, he smiled and said, "You got a pretty good set of choppers," then he added, "for somebody your age." It was the same after the hearing test-"Your hearing is not bad-for somebody your age." The eye doctor said the same thing. Even my regular doctor, a man I've known all my life, called me in to review my test results. My blood pressure was good — for a man my age; my cholesterol was good — for a man my age. I scored well on every test-for a man my age!

This got me to thinking: just how old is old enough? Is there a point at which it would be better to just sort of fade away — or better yet to make a quick exit, particularly while doing something exciting like shooting a double on a covey rise of quail or right after easing into the boat a 20 ounce red bream boat that hit a popping bug on a five weight fly rod.

A few months later I was coon hunting. An old man, by old I mean old enough he could have been my daddy, and I came up out of the swamp onto the dam of a small pond. A bunch of boys, I guess they were young men, eighteen to twenty, something like that, were camping on the dam. They had a big fire and the old man and I went over to warm up.

The boys were engaged in a discussion about the very topic I had been contemplating. It seems someone they knew had died. He was eight-five years old. They seemed completely insensitive to the old man as one said, "Well, it was time for him to go." Another asked, "Why would anyone even want to live that long?" Finally one said, "I just don't think I want to live to be eighty-five!"

About that time there was a break in the talking and the old man spoke: "The reason none of you boys want to live to be eighty-five is none of you have ever been eighty-four!"

I chuckled outwardly and smiled deep inside. I didn't have the answer to my question as to how old was old enough, but I had part of it. If you can be coon hunting, or whatever else you like to do at eighty-four, then eighty-five is not old enough. I think I'll just wait about another quarter century to contemplate that question again.

Remembering Jim

It was Christmas Eve, almost midnight, nearly time for Santa to be making his rounds. I was already in bed when the phone rang. It was Jim.

"Gary", he said excitedly, "I need a goat-a billy goat!"

"Jim", I replied," what in the H ... are you talking about?"

With an earnest tone he came right back," I need a billy goat.

I've waited to the last minute and I need a billy goat for my stepson. It's the only thing he wants for Christmas. I knew you could help me."

The Jim calling me was Jim Nelson, a fellow lawyer. I knew he was putting me on, but I wasn't quite sure. He was doing the same thing to me he did so effectively with juries. He kept on so pleadingly, so insistently, that in spite of his story being absurd, I still had doubts about whether it was true and whether he really did need a billy goat.

Several years later, on a Sunday morning, I would get a call from Jim's secretary. With a breaking voice her words came over the phone, "Gary, we lost Jim last night."

I hesitated then said, "Lost, what do you mean lost?" Of course I knew what she meant, but she had taken me by such surprise it was the only thing I could think to say. She explained Jim had fallen in his home, hit his head, and been killed.

When people tell me they can't afford to go to college, I think of Jim. Jim didn't graduate from high school. He dropped out, married, and soon had his first child. He joined the military as a way to support his family. While in the army he took advantage of school opportunities and got his GED. With an honorable discharge and his GED he was admitted to the University of North Carolina. He worked two jobs, one delivering the student newspaper, The Daily Tar Heel, before classes. His senior year he would go to a friend to borrow a sports coat, not being able to afford one himself, to wear to his installation into the Phi Beta Kappa Society.

Jim, now with two children, went on to law school at Carolina. Again, in spite of family responsibilities and working, he distinguished himself academically being on the editorial board of the Law Review.

Jim came home to Wilmington to begin practicing his profession at a salary of $100.00 a week. He associated himself with Aaron Goldberg, the city's most prominent criminal attorney at the time. When he got his first paycheck, Jim went straight to the bank, cashed his check, and drove to Parker's grocery. Jim said he went in, bought a quart of fresh squeezed orange juice, returned to the car and drank the whole quart there in the parking lot. It was the first time since he had been married he was able to afford fresh-squeezed orange juice.

Jim went on to achieve prominence as a lawyer. In addition to having one of the best reputations in North Carolina, he served the legal profession as a member of the Council of the North Carolina State Bar and an examiner with the Board of Law Examiners. He served as president of the Academy of Trial Lawyers. He was honored with membership in the International Society of Barristers. I could go on and on.

There are so many Jim Nelson stories. He was so full of life, he could find something humorous in even the most serious of situations, he understood people, and he really cared about those he represented, their problems.

I guess with the time limitations I can use his life to say to young people: if you really want to, if you are willing to work and sacrifice, you can get past financial difficulties to reach the opportunities life has to offer. You too can attain!

Jim Nelson was not just an extraordinary lawyer, he was an extraordinary human being. You are not born extraordinary. It is something you make of yourself.

Out Of Gas

Day was just breaking. Phil, my wife's uncle, and I had pulled up beside the truck of Jimmy the bait man. I had gone to Columbia to go striper fishing. Phil and Jimmy bantered back and forth as Jimmy dipped minnows from the large bait tank in the back of his truck and put them in Phil's live well.

Phil asked Jimmy if anyone was catching stripers. "You will need to go way down river," he replied. "They have been catching them with free floating minnows, but you need to go past the old pier."

We had fished the previous morning, but had stayed fairly close to the landing. We had not put a single striper in the boat and hoped this morning would be different. We had drinks, Nabs, Vienna sausage, suntan lotion. We had purchased some new plugs. Phil had even tuned the motor up from the day before. We were ready!

We both needed to be back at noon, but Jimmy's advice about going way down river was too tempting. We could make the run and still have three hours of fishing time. Just as we passed the pier the motor sputtered and then cut off. Phil pulled the cord until he had worked up a sweat, but the motor would not come back to life. He took the cover off and made some adjustments and pulled again. Not even a sputter.

Finally, he checked the gas tank. That's right. We had planned for everything except the most important — making sure the gas tank was full. Over the next four hours we sat on the river. We decided we might as well fish while we waited for help, threw out our lines, and actually caught six catfish.

Each time a boat would pass we would signal for them to come to us,explain our situation and ask if they had any spare gas. One man just laughed at us and motored on down the river. The others, however, seemed really concerned. Yet none had enough spare gas to get us back to the landing. One offered to stop fishing and tow us back to the landing. One gave us a half gallon, but we needed four or five gallons.

One young boy with an old, small ragged-looking boat, and to be truthful, the boy looked about as ragged as the boat,offered to take us to the landing, let us get gas, and bring us back.

A bulldozer cranked up on the hill just above us. We got the boat to the bank and Phil went to see if the operator might have some gas. About an hour later, after I had decided he had gotten lost, after I had imagined I would spend the night there on the bank, after I had figured how I would have to tell his children he had gone off it the woods and never returned, he came back with five gallons of gas.

The gas came from Marion Burnside, who I was later told was the richest man in Richland County. He was sitting in his jeep watching the bulldozer work when Phil went looking for gas. He took Phil about nine miles to his hunting lodge, got gas, brought him back and would not let us pay. He would not leave until he saw the boat would crank and we were going up river.

Returning home I thought about our day. Certain lessons came to mind:

(1)   You can concentrate on the small stuff so much you neglect the big things.

(2)   How nice a person is does not depend upon looks or money.

(3)   Most folks really do want to help folks in trouble and are sorry when they cannot.

(4)   A few folks think it's funny to see someone in trouble.

(5)   Even when you are in trouble, find something constructive to do — in other words, go ahead and fish.

(6)   If you have trouble it is nice to have a buddy with you: if you're alone, your imagination can run wild.

(7)   Getting home is as important as going, so be sure to check your gas tank.

One final thing; if any of you ever see Marion Burnside broken down beside the road, help him and send me the bill.

My Daddy Told Me

This Sunday is Father's Day. My daddy died over fifty years ago. I have children and grandchildren. When I look in the mirror I realize now I am more father and grandfather than son. When I think about my daddy, here are some of the things I remember he told me:

"There are things in life worse than death." He said this many times, but the time I remember most vividly was a time we were going to get a hamburger for lunch. Daddy had cancer and been told he had less than a year to live. I can still see him as he looked me in the face and said: "Son, I don't want to die, but I would rather go now than live in some rest home not being able to wait on myself. Existence is not living. There are worse things than dying."

"If you insist on getting your way in every little thing, you will find in time you will not get your way in the big things." This came up in the context of a man in the county who was a political power. This man became so important in his own eyes he thought whatever he wanted should be done without question. He became vindictive against anyone who opposed him. Daddy said, "Son, you watch, the time will come when whatever he wants people will oppose him just because he wants it." I've seen the truth of this over and over. A person hollers, screams, and pushes, whatever to get their way about things that are not really important. And then something that is really important comes along and no one pays any attention to what that person has to say.

One favorite saying of Daddy's was: "It's better to want something you do not have than to have something you do not want." Man, just think of all the folks you know who just had to have a boat! Just had to have one! Then it turned out to be a cash drain and they could not wait to get rid of it, but could not come close to getting their money back. I've known people who wanted political offices, who once elected wished they could give their positions to someone else. The list goes on and on-big houses, fame, position, horses — you get the picture.

"Don't let what people say make you mad." This was another of Daddy's oft given advices. He explained it to me this way. "If a friend of mine says something to me I do not like — I say to myself. He is a friend of mine. He must be having a bad day or he would not have said something like that. I'll look over it because I have bad days, too. If someone I do not know or someone I do not particularly like says something hateful or ugly to me, then I say to myself-Ha, he probably thinks that is going to upset me. Why am I going to let someone I don't know or don't like make me mad? If I do that I am letting them control me.

"Live your own life." This advice came one night when I went with Daddy to a company fish fry. I had just graduated from undergrad school. Several of the high company officials were advising me as to what I should do with my life. As soon as we got in the car to go home Daddy told me to pay little attention to what the officials had been telling me. He said I had to live "my life!" Other times he explained it this way: If you do in life what you want and it does not work out, you have only yourself to blame. If you do with your life what you think others want you to do and it does not work out, then you blame them." In the first instance even if life has not been everything you wanted, you are still left with the satisfaction of having been in control, to some extent at least, of your own destiny. If you allow others to dictate the course of your life and life is not what you want, you are often left bitter and disillusioned, not only with life, but also at those who directed the course of your life.

Daddy told me a lot of other stuff, some of it too personal to share.

The Obligation To Witness

The requirement we witness to the world is well illustrated in the Bible. Perhaps Jesus himself is the best example in that he would leave heaven to personally come, live among us; and by example and teachings show us how we should live.

In Luke's Gospel in the 12th chapter at the eighth verse Jesus tells the people: "And I tell you, everyone who acknowledges me before men, the Son of Man will also acknowledge before the angels of God."

And in the first chapter of Acts, just before Jesus ascends to the Father, he says to those standing there: "and you shall be my witnesses in Jerusalem and in all Judea and Samaria and to the end of the earth."

While holding court in Lumberton I saw the requirement to witness fulfilled in a way that has had a lasting impression on me. We were getting ready to try a man for possession of drugs. As we prepared to select a jury his lawyer stood up and said the man wanted to plead guilty. As part of the process of taking his plea I asked him if he wanted to say anything before I sentenced him.

The man stood and in a quivering voice related how he started using drugs recreationally. How he graduated from what some call "soft" drugs to "hard" drugs, chiefly crack cocaine. He told of having a wife and child, having a good job and a house. All lost because of drugs. He told of trying to get treatment. He had gone to the Department of Social Services, the hospital and even the Sheriff's department trying to get help. Social Services told him they had no drug programs. The hospital could not help unless he had money or insurance. The Sheriff's department could do nothing as he had not broken the law.

He stood before me saying he did not care what I did as long as he could get help. Because of the amount of the drugs, the guidelines I work under required I give him an active prison sentence.

Since he plead guilty we did not need the jury and I told them they could go. One juror stayed. When court was over he came and asked the bailiff if he could speak with me. He asked me if it was possible for him to talk with the man I sentenced for drug possession before he was sent from the local jail to prison. He wanted to tell him about Jesus.

I have often thought of how I sat up there on a raised dais, wearing the black robe symbolizing the authority of the judiciary, with an American flag on one side and a North Carolina flag on the other, the symbols of the power of our nation and state, with a uniformed deputy with a gun standing on both sides of my bench ready to carry out my orders. Yet, the only thing I could do for a man imprisoned by drugs was to send him to a prison of steel bars. Yet this Christian layman saw this tragedy as an opportunity to share Jesus.

All prisons do not have steel bars. Some people are imprisoned by substance abuse like the man I just told you about. Some people are imprisoned by illnesses which confine them or prevent them from doing what they would like. Some are imprisoned by loneliness. Some are imprisoned in nursing homes. Some people are imprisoned by their own consuming emotions of anger or ill will toward others.

Just this week I heard of a young woman who felt herself imprisoned by a troubled marriage. She went to a Christian counselor. She related to the counselor how her husband had hurt her with words and things he had done during the past couple of years. The counselor advised the young woman that her use of the word "hurt" was in the language of psychologists a code word for anger. The woman was still mad at her husband, but by using the word "hurt" she was shifting all responsibility and fault for the broken the relationship to the husband. In other words, there was nothing she could do about being hurt, but to admit she was still harboring anger over past deeds was to admit she was not forgiving.

You may know people who are imprisoned by some of these things. In Mathew Jesus talked about being in prison and being visited and being in prison and not being visited. When you visit someone who is sick, or lonely, or in the nursing home, or someone who suffers from depression brought on by the inability to dispel unhealthy emotions, surely you are visiting those imprisoned as much so as a visit to those behind steel bars. When your life's journey is over, you are likely to hear Jesus say: "As oft as you did it to one of the least of these my brethren, you did it to me."

We often make the mistake of thinking witnessing counts only when we are witnessing to the unsaved. But for those of us who are believers, when life comes against us in hard and often cruel ways, we need the witness of our brothers and sisters to remind us of the love and power of Jesus.

God's Witness

Cecil Sherman in Foundations Commentary says: "It would seem to me something as important as the resurrection announcement would be entrusted to Peter or John, maybe Andrew or Philip or James, one of the important people in the disciple band. But as is so often true in the New Testament, someone came out of the back rank of the disciples and to that relatively obscure believer was given the honor of announcing the great miracle and the great hope of the Church. Of all people, it was Mary Magdalene who made the announcement that Jesus was risen .... "

When I think of how unlikely a candidate Mary Magdalene was as the first witness to the resurrection, I think of an encounter I had with another unlikely, or I thought unlikely witness, to the risen Lord. It was a Maundy Thursday and I was holding court in Jacksonville, North Carolina.

It was a bad case. A man was accused of molesting his three- year old stepdaughter. He had been in jail nineteen months awaiting trial. The District Attorney offered to allow him to plead to an offence for which I could not give him more than sixteen months. If convicted by the jury, I was required by law to sentence him to no less than sixteen years in prison. Take the plea and go free that day. Go to trial and if convicted be sent to prison for at least sixteen years. He maintained his innocence and would not plead. His decision had to make you wonder about his guilt.

There is a woman lawyer in the town by the name Georgann. She is Greek. I have since we first met taken a liking to her. My attraction has been the show of real caring about her clients. Also, Georgann is a character. For several years she would meet a man in some city in the world and spend the weekend with him. Just like in the movie, "Same Time Next Year". She would not know where they were going until she received the plane tickets the week she was to fly out. Once when I was there holding court she showed me a ring and said: "'This is what I got for being really, really bad." She was living with a man to whom she was not married.

I have known Georgann for many years. While neither of us is old-old, we both are old. The time had come to instruct the jury and I had gone to my car to get some books and was going back to the courtroom. I must have looked as if I had the weight of the world on my shoulders. Georgann was walking toward me on a parallel sidewalk about thirty feet away. Suddenly she shouted at me: "'Gary-Christ is risen!'" With the exaltation she extended her arm and gave me the thumbs-up sign.

I returned the smile and shouted back: "Indeed He has, indeed He has." I extended my arm and gave the thumbs- up sign.

I watched as an old sinner, one who probably disappoints God every day, one whom the church certainly would not entrust to carry an important message, shuffled on with grey hair and slightly bent shoulders carrying a beat- up old briefcase to visit someone in jail. Someone few in the world cared about and most would just as soon never have to hear about. As long as they did not hear they would not have to face the depravity and ugliness of the world.

As she went another old sinner, with white hair and a gait not as steady as it was once, one who disappoints God daily, headed with his books back to the courtroom. Two old sinners going about the tasks they had undertaken. Two old sinners who live their lives with the sure hope that through the blood of Jesus they have eternal life. Two old sinners going about their tasks with full confidence that Christ is Risen.

Is not God marvelous? Just when we are at our lowest, just when we feel the weight of the world upon us, He sends a witness to remind us that Christ is risen.

Lessons Learned By A Newspaper Boy

I did two stints as a newspaper boy for the Star News. The first time was during the seventh grade. Back then the Star News had an afternoon edition which I delivered in Burgaw on my bike. My second stint was the year I was a freshman at Wilmington College, 1963-64. That time I delivered the morning paper from a French Renault for which my daddy had paid $125.00.

Looking back on those times I realize I learned some "life lessons" from my brief employment with the Star News. Some of them were pretty important and have kept me from making some serious mistakes later in life. Others, well, may be not so important have helped me just the same. Here are a few of them:

One: Just because a dog looks like Lassie does not mean he will not bite you! A large collie dog would chase me on my bike every time I passed a particular house. The owner assured me he was friendly and would not bite. Teeth marks in the calf of my leg proved otherwise. A water gun filled with ammonia solved the problem.

Two: Just because a man has a reputation as a respectable citizen does not mean he will not be slow to pay! Back then the paper was 35cents a week and I collected on Saturday afternoon. This one man invariably would pull out a twenty dollar bill and declare it was the smallest thing he had. After about the third time I told Daddy. He said: "Stay at the house." In a few minutes he was back with change for a twenty and instructions for me to go back and collect. When I told the man I had brought change for a twenty, he reached in his pocket and gave me the 35cents. There are some people who will make a game out of giving you a hard time, but if you ever beat them they will not play anymore.

Three: Even in the best of businesses, there is going to be some rain! As I told you, I delivered the paper the first time from a bike. Ever so often we would be having a rain storm, but the papers still had to be delivered. Often when this happened I would find my Daddy, who had a flexible work schedule, home waiting to take me on my rounds in the car. He also took me, as he did my older brother who was a paper boy before me, on our Sunday morning route. There was not a Sunday afternoon edition and the customers who subscribed to the evening edition got the Sunday Star News in the morning. No matter how independent you might like to be, nothing beats good parents when a rainy day comes.

Four: If you let a customer get behind in paying, you just may lose them! 35 cents a week does not seem like anything now, but remember Cokes were a nickel and you could get four gallons of gas for a dollar. A few customers, not many really, would put you off when you came to collect with some excuse or simply not come to the door even though you knew they were home. I developed the "three week you bring it to me" rule. If I did not get my money for three weeks, I quit delivering them a paper. Often they would call the house wanting to know where their paper was. Mama, who usually answered the phone at our house, would just tell them: "Bring the boy his money and he will bring you your paper." I had to pay the Star News whether I collected or not. I found out it was better to cut my losses quickly than to keep delivering papers to customers who were not going to pay. I could have had every household in Burgaw as a customer if I did not require them to pay.

Five: A little public relations can go a long way! Before I would begin the deliveries of my morning route, I would go by and give the policeman a paper. Figuring he was reading the paper made me a little careless stopping at stop signs. One morning he said: "Gary, you need to quit running stop signs or I am going to be forced to give you a ticket." I knew he had not seen me go through a stop sign. Someone had ratted on me. And without good reason as I had not even come close to hitting anyone. There were not that many people up between five and six in the morning. I think I know who it was, but I have never been sure. There are some people in this world who just resent anyone getting a break, but if you are nice to people you will get them anyway.

Six: Getting up early can make you feel righteous! I had to get up before five in order to be able to complete my route and leave Burgaw in time to be at the college for an eight o'clock class. In the winter it would not be daylight when I started and I would witness the breaking of the dawn. You formed a little informal bond with the other folks who had to be out that time of day. As you would pass you wave to each other and smile that smile that says: "We have beaten the rest of the world up. While they are sleeping on their shirttails, we are getting ahead. Are we not just a little superior?" There is a self-confidence and, yes, a little feeling of self-righteousness that comes with beating most of the other people up. Maybe it is not justified, but it still feels good.

These lessons and others I learned while a Star News newspaper boy have helped me in life. Lessons learned early are often the most beneficial as you get to apply them over a longer time.

Letter To Alex

You are now a junior in High School. There are certain mile stones in life that are more important than others—or another way of saying it is that some years have more effect on your later years than others. The junior year in High School is one of those years. There are several reasons for this. One is that the grades you make this year will have a greater impact on you getting into a college of your choice than any other. Your college applications will go in next fall before senior grades are available. It is your last chance to build an impressive extra-curricular resume to include with your college application.

The year is important for other "out of school" reasons. You now have your drivers' license and the added freedom, and hopefully the added responsibility, that goes with that. Another is that your thoughts begin to turn to what you want to do after high school and even after college. Another is girls—relationships take on a more adult seriousness than before. In North Carolina you are now considered an adult for criminal law purposes—so things that before might have been considered childish pranks or just part of growing up are now taken seriously. Still another is that you will begin to establish habits that may last your lifetime.

I am an old man and naive in many of the ways the world operates today. Yet, I believe the suggestions I'm about to give you are valid to help you avoid mistakes and make your life more meaningful between your age and mine.

No. 1: LEARN A SECOND LANGUAGE. I mean learn it to the point you can communicate with someone in that language and not just enough to pass a course in school. I would suggest Spanish. One reason is over 15% of the United States population is Hispanic and they are not all going to learn English. It is usually the third generation before families abandon their native language for that of their new country. Not only are they going to be in the work force, but you will encounter them in almost every aspect of life. Even if they can speak English, it would be good to be able to know what they are saying when they are speaking in Spanish to another person of Hispanic descent. If you learn a language and do not use it, you will lose it. Your opportunity to use Spanish in this country is greater than any other foreign language. The most important reason for you to learn Spanish is that it will allow you to be nice to a group of people that are often marginalized. If you grow in your Christian faith, and I hope you do, in may allow you to witness your faith. I find it very ironic when I hear professing Christians say, usually in a hateful tone: "If they can't speak English they just ought to go back where they came from!" I believe the better attitude is that if they cannot speak English maybe I can help them learn. When you see a person who cannot speak English, I want you to think about this: How bad would your life have to be for you to leave your homeland, most of your family, and go to a place where you could not understand the people, you could only get a low paying job, and lots of people look down on you? You can brighten these people's lives by being able to speak to them in their language.

No. 2: BEGIN NOW TO CONTROL YOUR WEIGHT: No, you do not have a weight problem, but just think—two pounds a year for the next 20 years and you are forty pounds overweight. You do not notice two pounds a years—after all that is less than three ounces a month. Learn the habit of exercise. Do vigorous exercise at least 30 minutes five days a week. Drink water instead of soda (or as my granddaddy would have called it: belly wash). Pay attention to calories. If you want to weigh 175 pounds—you can take in 2625 calories a day. Anything over, unless used up by exercise and you gain weight. Why is this so important? Because overweight brings on heart problems, diabetes and other health issues. In addition it limits your ability to participate in many activities—both fun and work related. A man with a big belly can watch sports on TV. A man in shape can play sports! A man with a big gut can sit in an office. A man in shape can sit in an office or lead an expedition! It is patriotic—overweight people are one of the main reasons our nation's health care system costs more than most any other industrialized nation in the world. Having said all this—do not judge overweight people too harshly. Many have reasons for being so beyond not caring and lack of discipline.

No. 3: GO TO CHURCH: I know your parents go to church. I also know they do not go as often as they should. You have your driver's license—you do not have an excuse for not going. I suggest you attend a different church at least once a month for a year. Go to a church with traditional worship style, go to one with contemporary worship style, go to one with a formal liturgy (such as Episcopal), attend a Catholic Mass, go to a Jewish Synagogue, attend a large non-denominational community church, attend a predominately black church, etc. I think you will find God in all of them. However, you may find God speaks to you more in one than another. This may change in time and God may lead you in a different direction and to a church family different than the one that appeals now. One way to evaluate a church is the opportunities it gives you. I have heard people say church is not about you—I would disagree to an extent. It is about you in the sense that it should provide you with the opportunity to grow in your faith, to bond with other believers, to engage in meaningful worship, and the opportunity to serve others. The opportunity to serve others is the most important. There is no higher form of worship than helping the less fortunate. Remember—the best Christian is not necessarily the one who knows the most about the Bible, has the most education, or the one who holds the highest church offices (including the preacher). It is the one who tends to the less fortunate and downtrodden! Be careful of show business, feel good churches. Be careful of churches where the minister is the primary focus. Be careful of churches that preach love, but have hateful attitudes toward those who are different.

No. 4: DO NOT DATE SILLY GIRLS (I will later give this advice to my granddaughters about dating silly boys): Remember there is a difference between "fun loving" and silly. Fun loving people are often those who want to get the most out of life, who take the time and make the effort to get the most out of any occasion. Silly people, on the other hand, think they are entitled to be entertained all the time. They are usually self-centered and want to always be the center of attention. They seldom see any seriousness in life and fail to prepare for tomorrow. They often disdain ambition and make fun of education. They see hard work as a fool's activity. I cannot exactly define what I mean by a silly person, but you will know them after being around them for a little time. Date girls who want their life to amount to something. Girls who are looking further down the road than the Friday night ballgame. I married a serious, fun loving girl and it has been one of the two best decisions I have ever made.

No. 5: LEARN TO PLAY GOLF AND TENNIS: Your granddaddy does not play golf and did not like it when he did. He did play "at tennis" for a number of years. As you know I like to fish and hunt. However, a lot more people play golf than hunt and fish. If you pursue a career in business, you will find a lot of decisions and contacts are made on golf courses. If you pursue any other profession you will still find many relationships are formed and enhanced on golf courses. Your granddaddy is a loner and sometimes that is not good. I have served on a college board, the Council of the North Carolina State Bar, as a member of the Conference of Superior Court Judges and other such. During down time other members of these groups played golf and the bonds and friendships established benefited them and the organizations. As for tennis, I just like it. It allows you to compete as an individual or as a member of team. It is a sport you can play the better part of your life. Look around—most any town of any size you see will have a country club with a golf course and tennis courts. Look to see who the members are—the movers and shakers will be there. Just because you want to associate with members of these groups does not mean you are a snob—though it could as there are often a lot of snobs at these places. Most of the members are good people who are the most active in the community life of their town.

No. 6: GO ON A MISSION TRIP: Why? You need to see the face of poverty! I was privileged growing up to spend summers with my grandparents in an area with a lot of poverty. The woman who cooked and cleaned for us (my grandmother was confined to a wheel chair) lived in a house without running water or electrify. The same was true of the family of my best friend there. When it rained their well would be muddy and they would come to our house for water which they had to carry a half mile back to their house. The adults in these families could not read or write. They were some of the best people I have ever known. My grandparents were better off, but not by much. The experience of living those summers in that environment has impacted my view of the world more than I can ever explain. I am greatly blessed to have had it. While I have never desired great wealth, I learned I did not want to be poor or uneducated.

There is poverty where you live, but poverty in the United States is often hidden and disguised by such things as school lunches that lead the better off to believe it does not exist. The stigma of poverty causes those in poverty to often not ask for or take advantage of programs that could help.

In your life you may have the opportunity to make significant income. If you do, remember that with opportunity comes responsibility. You will begin to make money through part time jobs. You are not too young to follow my 10-10-80 rule. You give away 10%, you save 10% and do what you want with the 80%. The talent to make money is just as God given as the talent to make music or art or speak to crowds. If you are given that talent, you should share a portion of that income with the less fortunate. That may mean sharing with the undeserving and unlovable. Be able to say with St. Francis: "I ask not to be loved, but to be able to love!"

So, get your best girl and your best bud and volunteer for a Habitat for Humanity project this year. Volunteer at a soup kitchen. Seek the opportunity to go on a mission trip to a third world country next summer. Your view of the world and people will be forever changed.

No. 7: LIVE A FULFILLING LIFE: What it takes to accomplish this varies with people. What may be fulfilling to me may be boring and of little consequence to you. A friend of mine once told me to be happy a person needs to follow their passions. If you can find your passion follow it without regard to whether it will make you the most money. Realize that passions change over time. For twenty-five years I was passionate about practicing law. I lost that passion. I have been for the past twenty years passionate about being a judge, but that passion too has passed. I am now ready to pursue a new passion.

My daddy told me to be my own person. Don't try to be what your parents (or your granddaddy) want you to be. Daddy said: "Son, if you try to be what others want you to be and it does not work out, it will leave you bitter. If you try to be what you want and it does not work out, you are left with the satisfaction of having tried without the bitterness. Plus you are more likely to pick yourself up and go on to something else rather than wallowing in your misery".

No 8: READ A NEWSPAPER: Yes, you can get the news and find out what is going on in the world from television and computer pop-ups. However, from my observation television has gotten too slanted. They give opinions as news. You need to know the facts before you start forming your opinion. Newspapers are the best source for this. Most papers tell you when they are giving opinions and when the story is relaying the facts. Of course the editors may have a point of view that influences how they write, but most often you know it and can compensate for it. Many, if not most, of the people I know do not read a newspaper. However, the smartest and best informed people I know do.

Read the headlines on the front page and then at least scan the sto-

ries that interest you. Do the same for the local section so you will know
what is going on in your community. Do the same for the sports section. While I seldom read the sports section it is good to do so as most
anywhere you go people will be talking about the latest in the sports
world. Your granddaddy always reads the comics and reads them last,
even if he neglects some of the other sections. That way I leave home
with a smile on my face and not too depressed by all the other stuff I
have just read. If you want I will subscribe to an online edition of your
local paper for you.

No. 9: GET INVOLVED IN A POLITICAL COMPAIGN: Again, get
your best girl and best bud and volunteer to work in a political cam-
paign. This next year will be a great year for doing that with all the election campaigns in full swing. Why should you do this? Because who
holds public office will affect your life. It is extreme ignorance to believe
elections do not matter. Volunteer to work at a headquarters a couple
of nights. Volunteer to be a poll worker after school on election day. I
am not going to suggest a candidate to you. You look into what they
stand for and the race that will have the greatest impact on you. It may
not be a national or state race—it may be a local race. Good citizenship
demands you be politically informed and often involved. You are not
too young to begin.

No. 10: SOME SHORT SUGGESTIONS AND WARNINGS:

Sex can result in fatherhood;

Alcohol is an enhancer, never the main event;

Drugs are illegal and can keep you out of college, a good job, or a
good peer group;

Never, ever, hesitate to let others know of your Christian faith;

Negativism is contagious—do not spend much time with negative people;

Girls parents (as well as other elders) like politeness;

How you dress does matter;

Learn at least the first verse of "The Star-Spangled Banner", "God Bless America", "Silent Night" and "Joy to the World".

Good table manners may not be noticed, but bad ones are;

It is better to be respected than liked;

Do not judge others, but do judge yourself.

Hope to see you soon.

Lots of Love!

Granddaddy

.

Acknowledgments

I have always liked watching and listening to people. Maybe it's a middle child thing. I was sandwiched between two of the best brothers a fellow could have. They were different from each other, and me, to the point that, except for some physical characteristics, one would not think we had the same mama and daddy. I was always jealous of their names. Ross was named for our daddy and Bill was named for our granddaddy—two men that no matter what I accomplish, I will never live up to. I never liked my name, yet I gave it to my son. At least he does not have as much to live up to as my brothers living up to their names.

Ross, my big brother, was a big storyteller. Most of the time his stories had some element of truth, which he embellished. Many of his stories were complete fabrications but told with such sincerity that you were not sure whether they were true or not. When he wanted to impart some tidbit of wisdom to me, he would start by saying: "Buba, let me tell you something." An example was once when he turned his ankle and was on crutches. He stayed on those crutches two weeks longer than he needed because the girls at school would cater to him and carry his books. Ross told me: "Buba, let me tell something. If you can ever get a girl thinking you need her, she will do anything you ask. As long as I am on these crutches it is—'Ross, let me get the door. Ross let me carry those books.' The minute I lay them down I am supposed to be doing for them." Ross made it just a little pass a half century before we lost him. He lived most of that time in the left lane. Whatever Ross did, he wanted to do big.

Bill, my little brother, is different. While Ross was fun to listen to, Bill is fun to watch. You are never quite sure what Bill might do next. Bill has that talent for working people to get them to do what he wants with them thinking it was their idea. It is a talent he honed working mama. Let me tell you, if you knew our mama you would know that working her was no easy proposition. Yet, Bill had little difficulty getting his way. Bill told me early on he felt some religious calling, but it was not for the pulpit. Watching the twists and turns his life took before he landed as head of the Bishop Gadsden Retirement Community in Charleston, South Carolina makes one know an other than human force was directing his life. Like Ross, Bill lives life big, just in a different way.

As you can see by me telling you about my brothers, family loams big in my life. I learned so much about life from my daddy and mama. My grandparents played huge roles in shaping my life values and viewpoints. When I married my wife's family just took me in as if I had always been in their family. One of my big "hopes" in life is that after I am gone my children will continue to whole family close.

Stories, stories, stories—if you like stories you should have worked at Futch's Esso in Burgaw like I did growing up. Futch's Esso was the meeting place for the men in Burgaw. Burgaw is a small town and if you have ever lived in one you know there are no secrets—everybody knows everybody's personal life and what's furthermore they want to tell you what they know. In those days kids did not participate in the conversations of adults, they sat to the side and listened.

During the first years I practiced law I would most morning visit

Durham Drug Store before going to the office for coffee. Durham Drug was like Futch's Esso as it was a town gossip center. The big difference was that Futch's was a men's meeting place and Durham's had a mixed male and female clientele. It was fun to watch and listen to how the same tale was told and received at the two places. For instance, let's say it was discovered a couple in town were engaged in an affair. At Futch's the story would be told with lots of grinnig and laughter. At Durham's the men might smile slightly with their heads down, but the women would be shaking their heads and displayed scorned, disgusted looks, but still looks that said: "Tell me more, tell me more!"

You cannot be a good lawyer unless you are a good listener. The same goes for being a good judge. A lawyer has to not only hear what his client is saying but also what he is not saying. A judge has to listen to the witness, but also realize that most of the time he is not getting the full story. I spent a quarter of a century listening to stories as a lawyer and almost that long listening to stories as a judge. The stories I have heard during my nearly half century in the legal profession are in the thousands. I have seen human nature at his best and at its worst.

The stories I am telling you in this book come from the sources I have set out above. I am only telling you twenty-five from the thousands I have heard and lived and observed. Most, but not all, I first wrote and performed for WHQR Public Radio in Wilmington, North Carolina. I have to thank WHQR as the opportunity to do commentary on the radio forced me to put pen to paper and write.

I would not be telling you these stories except for a woman. She is a woman I have lived with for over fifty years. I guess the importance of her in my life was best summed up by my brother Ross. We were sitting in a bar in Destin, Florida looking out at the Gulf waters when, right out of the blue, he turned to me and said: "Buba, do you realize that if you had not married the woman you did you would be so sorry mama would not claim you?' My wife, Jennings, says it's a lie—that my mama would always claim me. However, the boy with whom I shared a bedroom for the first thirteen years of my life and was my confidant for many more knew some things Jennings still does not know and I hope she never knows. From the time we said "I do" in Moore's Creek Baptist church on that August afternoon in 1967 she has supported, encouraged, and challenged me to be the best I could be. She has been a far, far better wife than I have been a husband. If you asked her if that was true I expect she would say no, but I suspect deep down she knows it to be the truth. One of the most important ways she has supported me is by letting me be "me." I hope I have returned the favor by letting her be "her." I think it is in doing so that our "we" has been so strong and special.

I also would not be telling you these stories except for another woman, Kimberly Daniels Taws. Kimberly and I connected through the efforts of a friend of mine, John Vernon, who is the friend of a friend of Kimberly. He arranged for us to meet at his beach house and we immediately hit it off. There is no way not to like Kimberly. She is so positive in this time of negativity. She is less than half my age and has that quality of youth that sees the world as opportunity. Yet, you only have to talk with her a short time to see the realism that exists beneath the idealism. Shortly after reading the manuscript she agreed to publish through her business, The Country Book Shop, in Southern Pines, North Carolina. She has exhibited confidence in me and I have confidence in Kimberly.

Although you could, it is my hope you will not read all these stories in one sitting. I hope that after you read one you will sit the book down

for a while and ponder the story. Isn't "ponder" a great word? Ponder—
(define). Try to see what I saw. Try to hear what I heard. Try to learn
what I learned. And maybe, just maybe—you will find yourself or someone close to you in them.